Front Cover:
The grandeur, mystique and striking architecture of Fonthill are
captured in this intriguing photograph by Alan Karchmer © 1998.

Preface

Fonthill has fascinated America ever since tile magnate Henry Mercer built his unique home in 1908. Nearly 500,000 visitors have experienced its magic and Fonthill has become a National Historic Landmark. Fonthill has also been featured on television in an award-winning episode of "America's Castles."

Fonthill—The Home of Henry Chapman Mercer was first published in 1985.

This revised and expanded edition gives readers unique insights into Mercer and his magnificent residence. The new edition is distinguished by the addition of color photographs, architectural drawings and previously unpublished hand-drawn floor plans, artwork and comments from Mercer's own construction notebook on Fonthill.

We are indebted to David April, site administrator at Fonthill Museum, for his enthusiastic support in preparing the second edition. Special thanks are also extended to the many professionals, libraries and organizations whose contributions were invaluable.

Manor House Publishing

F·O·N·T·H·I·L·L

The Home of
Henry Chapman Mercer

An American
Architectural Treasure
By *Thomas G. Poos*

Second Edition, Revised and Expanded

MANOR HOUSE

Manor House Publishing Co., Inc.
Feasterville, Pennsylvania

Publisher's Cataloging-in-Publication
(Provided by Quality Books, Inc.)

Poos, Thomas G.
    Fonthill : the home of Henry Chapman Mercer :
an American architectural treasure / by Thomas G.
Poos. -- 2nd ed., rev. and expanded.
    p. cm.
    LCCN: 99-76288
    ISBN: 0-9645844-2-5

    1. Fonthill Museum. 2. Architecture, Domestic
--Pennsylvania--Doylestown. 3. Tiles--
Pennsylvania--Doylestown--History. 4. Historical
museums--Pennsylvania--Doylestown. 5. Gothic
revival (Architecture)--Pennsylvania--Doylestown.
6. Dwellings--Pennsylvania--Doylestown.
7. Mercer, Henry Chapman, 1856-1930.   I. Title.

NA7511.P4P66 2000   728.8'09748'21
           QBI99-500571

Printed in the United States of America

Library of Congress Catalog Card Number 99-076288

*"To the
dreams of man,
and what they lead
us to achieve…"*

The Saloon, and stairs leading up to the Gallery above doors to Entry Hall

Foreword

If you sit in one of the rooms of Fonthill for an entire day, you can see dramatic changes in sunlight and shadows on the walls, the columns, the nooks and crannies and the objects in the room. Changes in light transform rooms from dark, reflective spaces to bright, exciting spaces and, finally, to sparkling, magical spaces.

If you could stay at Fonthill for an entire year, you could see how the cool concrete surfaces give respite from the summer sun. You could watch the changing fall foliage from one of the many balconies. You could sit by the fire in the tower and listen to the winter winds. You could smell the green spring as the arboretum around the house begins to grow again.

If you could see all that has happened in Fonthill since construction was completed in 1910, you would see the colors of the walls gradually mellowing. You would see the trees in the arboretum and along the drive growing. You would see the tapestries on the walls and in the windows aging. You would see years of joy, study, reflection, melancholy, frustration and peace.

Fonthill changes every moment, every season, every year, but one thing about the house does not change — it is always a special place. It never recedes entirely into the background as simply an unnoticed environment. More frequently, in fact, it acts as a catalyst for whatever the visitor is doing — discovering, reflecting, enjoying, understanding. Only a few buildings can claim such specialness, and only a few of those are houses. Our role as visitors in such a place is to act to preserve that specialness.

The Saloon, and stairs leading up to the Gallery

Table of Contents

The Library – Richly decorated with tile, plus a balcony for private study

A Journey Past

The year is 1913. You are traveling north on Easton Road toward Doylestown, accompanying your good friend, John Wanamaker, on a visit to Fonthill, the recently built home of Henry Chapman Mercer, noted archaeologist, historian and ceramist.

As you roll along in his new motorcar, Wanamaker explains the reason for your visit. It seems that he is quite taken with the idea of decorating the fireplaces in his home with ceramic tile – the rage in interior design – and the finest examples of tilework that he's seen are those by Henry Mercer.

Wanting nothing but the best, he has requested Mercer tiles for his fireplaces. And to help him decide on a theme, Henry Mercer has graciously invited him to Fonthill to see designs created for previous customers, which the ceramist has incorporated into his own home. The invitation includes dinner as well, and Wanamaker assures you that Mercer has insisted that you stay over until morning before returning to Philadelphia.

It is a long drive, but at last you swing into the driveway leading up to Fonthill. As you pass slowly between two rows of young sycamore trees, the imposing structure looms ahead, resembling a cross between a Gothic mansion and a French chateau. From a distance, its gray color suggests weathered granite, but as you climb down from the automobile, a closer inspection reveals, instead, that the house is made entirely of concrete.

Fonthill's somewhat unusual appearance, however, pales quickly in comparison to what you discover inside. From the moment you enter, it's obvious that this is no ordinary country home.

Henry Mercer himself greets you at the door – he is a handsome man in his late fifties, with a full moustache – and

Above: The front of the Garage/Terrace Pavilion

Below: Rear view of the Garage/Terrace Pavilion, once an old barn

you follow in fascination as he leads you through his beloved Fonthill. It is at once both mysterious and exciting, filled with unexpected vistas and changes in level.

There are curved, vaulted ceilings reminding you of ancient castles. There are uniquely shaped rooms and alcoves connected by so many narrow passageways and winding staircases you could easily get lost for days. And all manner of niches and shelves are filled with ancient arti-facts, tools and pottery. The feeling is medieval, yet you also notice that the house boasts the latest electric lighting, modern plumbing and a central heating system.

And the tiles – everywhere there are tiles: set into the arches of the ceilings; on the walls and around windows; above and around fireplaces; on the floor and on the tops of built-in concrete vanities. They catch your eye with color and often tell a story. Why, there's even one room where the ceiling is completely covered with tiles depicting scenes of Columbus' discovery of the New World.

Later, after Wanamaker and Mercer have concluded their business, you are shown to your room. It is the Yellow Room, you are told, and there you start to dress for dinner. It takes longer than usual, however, for you can't help star-ing at the story of Bluebeard told in tiles on the wall. A noise like footsteps echoing nearby arouses your curiosity, but you dare not wander from your room for fear of losing your way in the maze of passageways.

Dinner is a sumptuous affair, served at a large table in the Saloon, the cavernous, two-story main room on the ground level.This is how, you imagine, the knights and nobles must have felt as they feasted in their castles. Over the main course, you ask Henry Mercer how he built such a remarkable home. While he explains, you look around with even greater appreciation at what this ingenious man has achieved.

Afterward, you adjourn to the library for brandy and cigars. There, you notice once again the motto, "Plus Ultra," inscribed in tile letters above the fireplace. From your study of Latin, you know that it means "More Beyond." How true, you think, remembering all that you've seen at Fonthill that day. How very true...

Henry Chapman Mercer

"He was building from the inside outward....and risked being responsible for a house which might terrorize the whole neighborhood."

W. T. Taylor in
The Architectural Record
March, 1913

2

A True American Dream

Earth mounds on platforms molded the ceilings; the forms for columns were made of boards.

A True American Dream

Henry Chapman Mercer began building Fonthill in 1908. Working exclusively with reinforced concrete – and with no machinery, no conventional blueprints, and very little measuring – the main structure of the house was completed in 1910. Finishing work continued until 1912, when – after spending an estimated $31,807–Mercer moved into his dream home.

And a dream home it was, in the truest sense of the word. From the first sketch to the last tile, Mercer built Fonthill entirely for himself, and entirely in his own manner.

Without formal architectural training, he created his own unique design from ideas inspired by his personal desires, memories of his travels, and scenes from prints or engravings. And he developed his own techniques – many worked out on the job – for constructing his design with concrete.

As a result, Fonthill is a highly personal, three dimensional testament to one man's inventiveness and artistic standards; to his courage in carrying out his convictions; and to his determination to build a house which would, in his own words, "Combine the poetry of the past with the convenience of the present."

In designing Fonthill – so named because of a natural spring on the site – Mercer drew heavily on his personal experiences. Born in 1856 to a wealthy Bucks County family, his youth was a privileged one. Private education, extensive travel abroad, a Harvard degree, and law school were his experiences before he turned to archaeology and anthropology. In the 1890s, he was appointed Curator of American and Prehistoric Archaeology at the Museum of the University of Pennsylvania. It was during these years that he began his collection of artifacts.

In 1897, Mercer began to experiment with pottery and ceramic tile production. By the turn of the century, he was successfully selling his decorative tiles. Decorative tiling was then in vogue, and Mercer, through his Moravian Pottery and Tile Works, became one of the best known suppliers.

His largest installation was the floor of the Pennsylvania State Capitol Building in 1904, but Mercer tiles were also used to decorate private residences and clubs throughout the country, from Philadelphia, New York, Boston, and Newport, RI, to as far west as San Francisco and Los Angeles. Mercer's records show, as well, that he supplied tiles for the U.S. Military Academy Chapel at West Point, and for homes in such far-flung places as Canada, England, France, Egypt and Cuba.

A major influence in Henry Mercer's life was his "Aunt Lela" – Elizabeth Chapman Lawrence, his mother's older sister. Elizabeth's husband, Timothy Bigelow Lawrence, was appointed Vice Consul General to Italy by Abraham Lincoln. During his youth, "Aunt Lela" brought Mercer to Europe on several occasions, and many of his ideas for Fonthill came from memories and sketches of buildings he saw during these early travels.

Elizabeth also financed his education, and supported all of Mercer's projects, both verbally and financially. She paid for his many trips, and even helped with expenses of establishing his first pottery and tile works.

Elizabeth Lawrence died in 1905, leaving Henry Mercer a share of her considerable fortune. In 1907, he inherited this money and began to design his dream house that same year. So ultimately, Elizabeth's money enabled Mercer to build Fonthill, as well as the new Moravian Pottery and Tile Works and the Mercer Museum.

In Fonthill, Mercer dedicated the Columbus Room to "Aunt Lela." Her initials appear on the columns of that room, and a poem to her memory runs around the ceiling in tile letters:

> *"Clay and rust in fire burnt bright*
> *For EL sake here flash the light."*

Fonthill's dramatic Conservatory

3

Room by Room, the Dream Unfolds

Mercer's plaster-of-Paris model of Fonthill (Front, above and Back)

Room by Room, the Dream Unfolds

Henry Mercer was 51 when he first considered building Fonthill during a visit to New England in the summer of 1907. Later that year he began to sketch out his ideas and develop his design.

Mercer planned the house from the inside out because, as he noted, "It was to be used first and looked at afterwards." Almost from the beginning, he intended Fonthill to be a museum as well as his personal residence, and displaying his collections of artifacts, prints and tiles was a major factor in his plans.

Mercer did not use conventional blueprints, but his notebook shows a considerable number of calculations and sketches of rooms and floor plans. He designed by first imagining a room and making rough sketches of each wall. He then cut the shape of the room out of a block of clay.

In this way, room by room, he wove his fantasies and his travel memories together. In his notes, for example, he tells us that "The arrangement of rooms at different levels seen over the gallery in the Saloon is a memory of a Turkish house seen by me from a rear garden in Salonica in 1886."

He also took suggestions from prints and engravings to plan the lighting in his rooms, and to achieve desired plays of light and shadow in the ceilings. Each room eventually had a name and a theme.

When all the rooms were modeled in clay, he placed the blocks on a table and assembled them into the interior arrangement he wanted. Suites were composed with regard for the relation of floor levels. Large stairways were avoided for economy of space, and irregular stairways and passages were made to conform to the arrangement of the suites.

At this point he had a general outline of the house, to which the roof was modeled. Only then did he turn his attention to the exterior, for the outside appearance of the house was of minor importance compared to the interior.

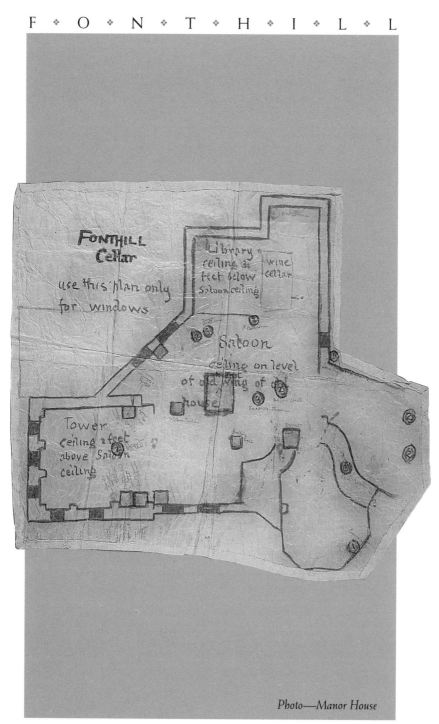

Mercer drew a plan for each level of Fonthill — his original plan for the Cellar is shown above. (Pencil and crayon on paper, linen, 28½"x 32")

The shapes of windows, rooflines, steeples and chimneys were established and refined. But these — and even the heights of walls — were, in his mind, just finishing touches.

Finally, he wrote, "After a good many changes in the profile of the tower, roofs, etc., a plaster-of-Paris model was made to scale, and used (as a working model) till the building was completed."

When finished, Mercer had created a model for a house that included 17 bedrooms, work rooms and living rooms plus eight full bathrooms and two lavatories. Another 13 rooms and two bathrooms were added with the building of the servants' quarters in 1910.

The basic organization is simple: the servants' area is separated from the main living area by the kitchen. Within the main part of the house, the Saloon is located on the same level as the kitchen for convenience in serving food, and sits in the base of the tower between the Morning Room and the Library. Above the Saloon, however, the rooms are freely positioned and shaped according to Mercer's desires and the need for support below.

No two of the rooms are similar in design. The stairways and passages, though well-lighted by windows, have many twists caused by their adaptation to different floor levels and room arrangements. And many of their suites are entirely isolated so that several families could conceivably live in the house without seeing each other.

Mercer created these isolated areas for a specific purpose. Since Fonthill was also to be a museum, he anticipated visitors moving through his home. In order to preserve his privacy, he arranged Fonthill's interior so he could close off certain rooms and go about his business undisturbed by people viewing his collections.

Fonthill as seen from East Court Street

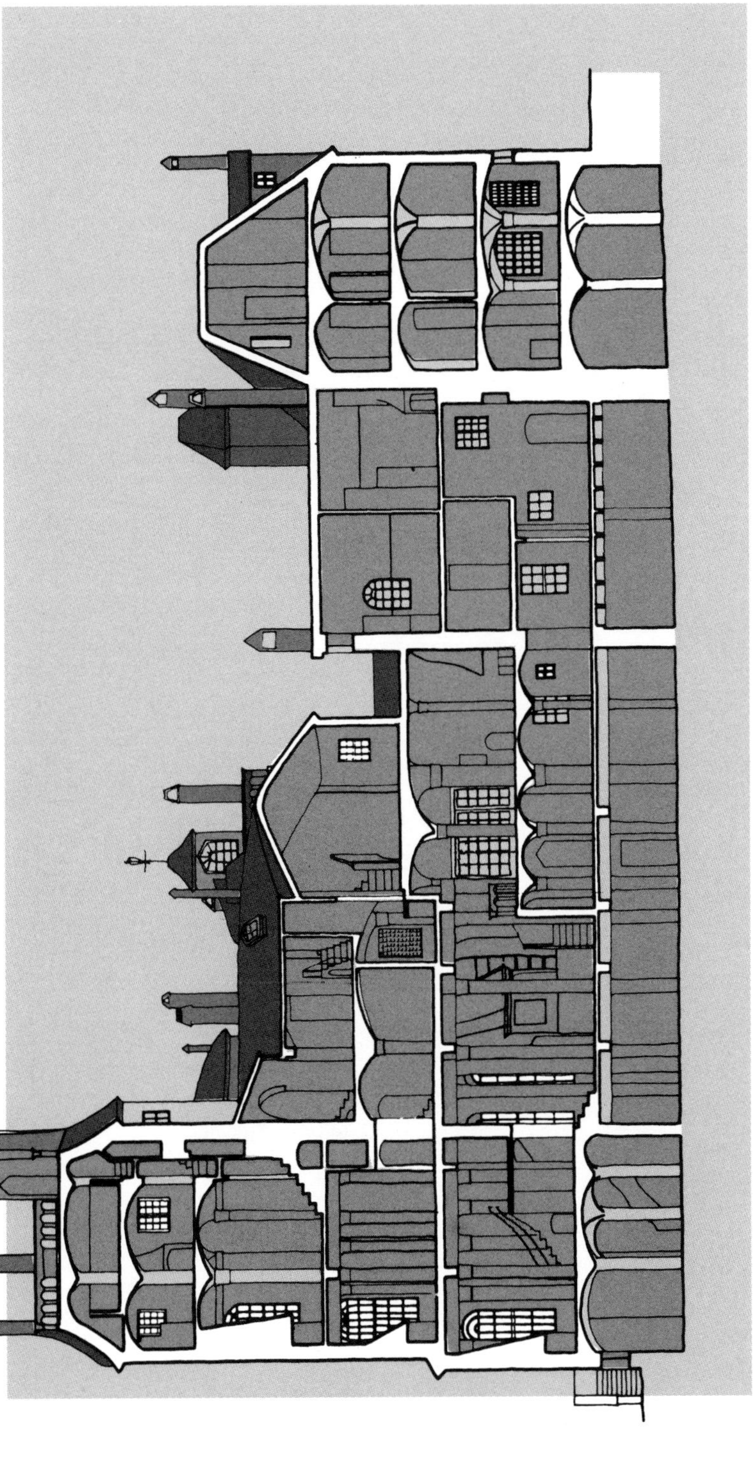

The cross sections and floor plans of Fonthill are courtesy of architect Kurt Eichenburger.

(Shading added to illustration above to provide depth)

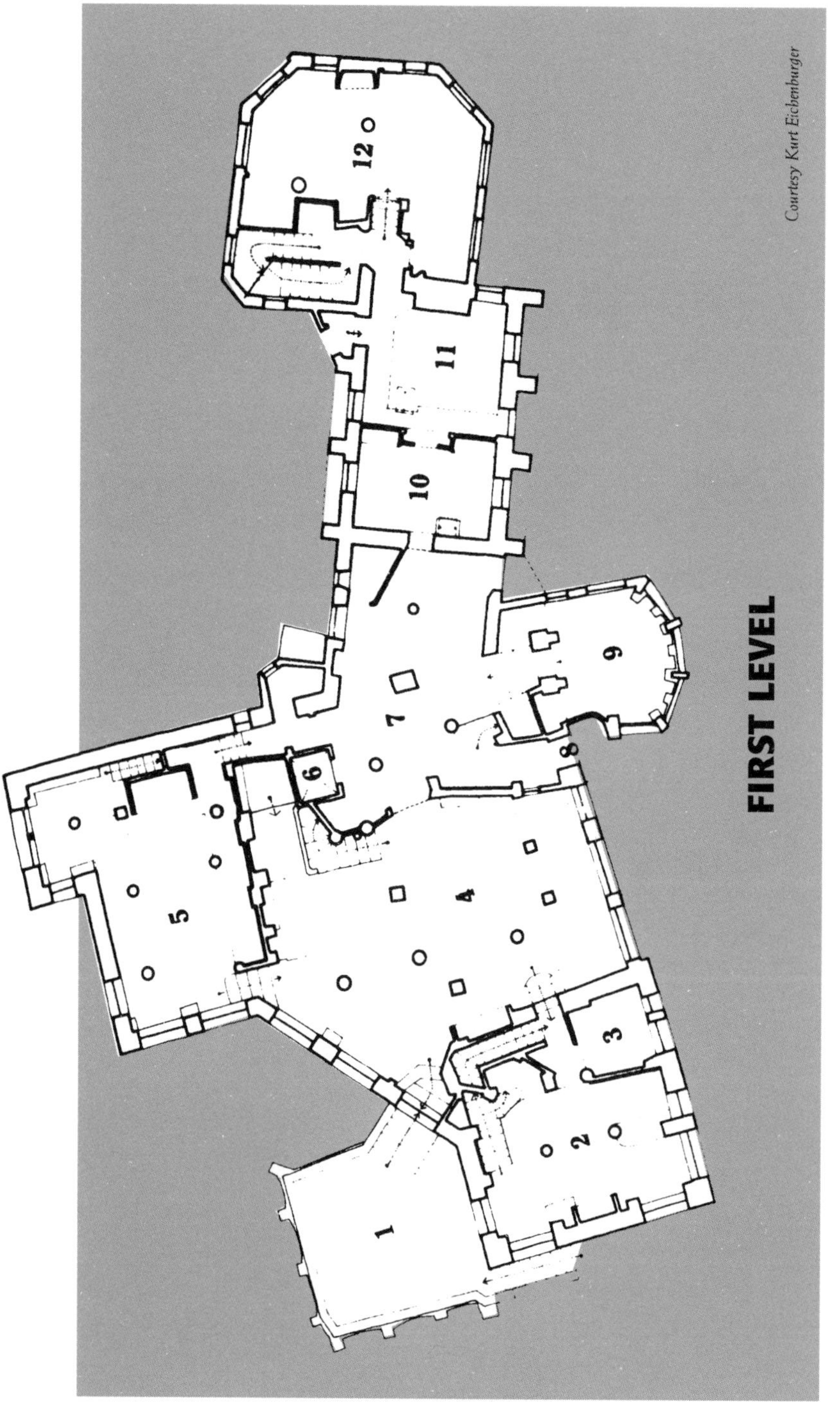

Courtesy Kurt Eichenberger

FIRST LEVEL

1. West Spring Terrace 2. Morning Room 3. Morning Room Bath 4. Saloon 5. Library 6. Second Level of Lift
7. Entry Hall 8. Front Door 9. Conservatory 10. Front Kitchen 11. Back Kitchen 12. Oven Room

Fonthill's First Level

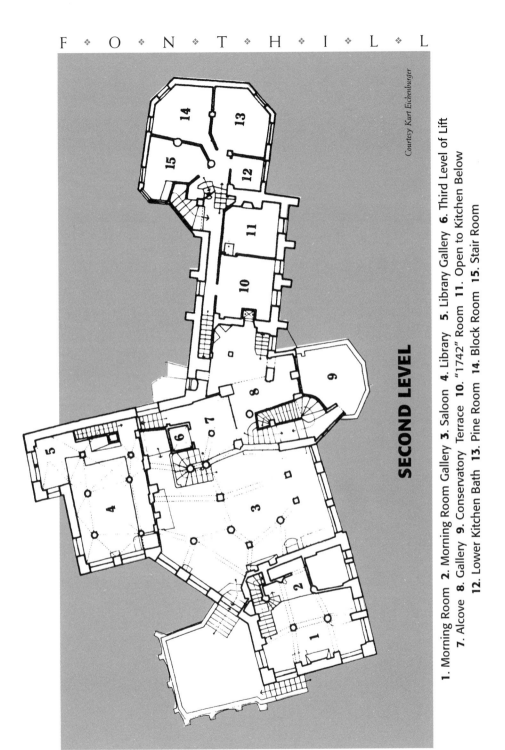

Courtesy Kurt Eichenlauger

SECOND LEVEL

1. Morning Room 2. Morning Room Gallery 3. Saloon 4. Library 5. Library Gallery 6. Third Level of Lift 7. Alcove 8. Gallery 9. Conservatory Terrace 10. "1742" Room 11. Open to Kitchen Below 12. Lower Kitchen Bath 13. Pine Room 14. Block Room 15. Stair Room

Fonthill's Second Level

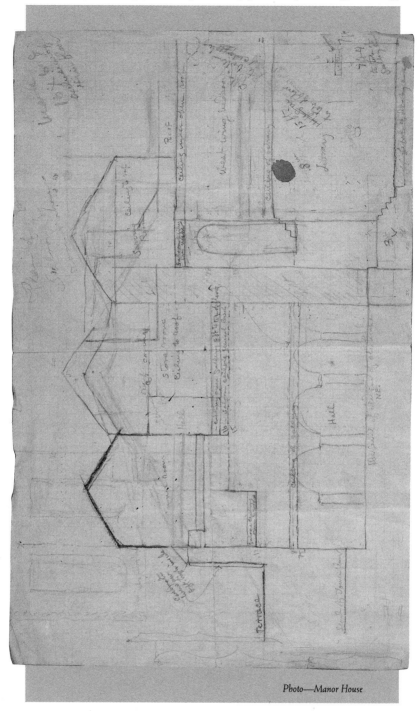

Photo—Manor House

Original hand-drawn cross section (pencil and crayon on paper, 11"x 17")

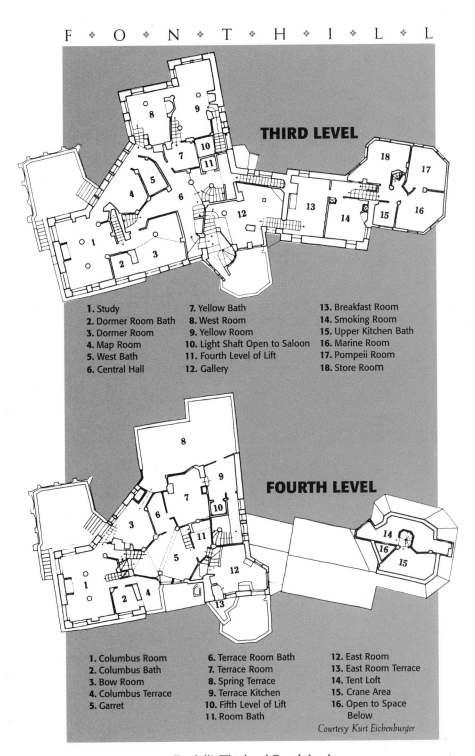

THIRD LEVEL

1. Study
2. Dormer Room Bath
3. Dormer Room
4. Map Room
5. West Bath
6. Central Hall
7. Yellow Bath
8. West Room
9. Yellow Room
10. Light Shaft Open to Saloon
11. Fourth Level of Lift
12. Gallery
13. Breakfast Room
14. Smoking Room
15. Upper Kitchen Bath
16. Marine Room
17. Pompeii Room
18. Store Room

FOURTH LEVEL

1. Columbus Room
2. Columbus Bath
3. Bow Room
4. Columbus Terrace
5. Garret
6. Terrace Room Bath
7. Terrace Room
8. Spring Terrace
9. Terrace Kitchen
10. Fifth Level of Lift
11. Room Bath
12. East Room
13. East Room Terrace
14. Tent Loft
15. Crane Area
16. Open to Space Below

Courtesy Kurt Eichenburger

Fonthill's Third and Fourth Levels

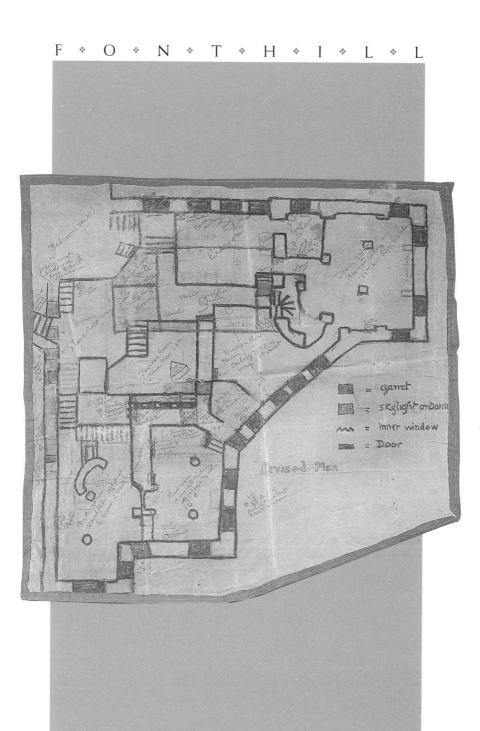

Photo—Manor House

Mercer's revised plan for the fourth level (charcoal on paper, 22½″ x 21½″)

38

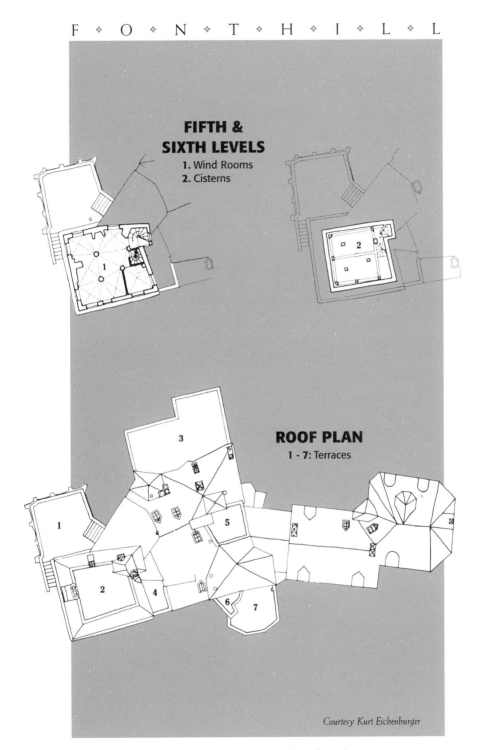

**FIFTH &
SIXTH LEVELS**
1. Wind Rooms
2. Cisterns

ROOF PLAN
1 - 7: Terraces

Courtesy Kurt Eichenburger

Fonthill's Fifth, Sixth and Roof Levels

4

Fonthill Comes to Life

Fonthill in early stages of construction

Fonthill Comes to Life

Fonthill is one of the first American buildings constructed of reinforced concrete. The first concrete was poured in March of 1908, and the basic construction of the main house was completed in three years.

Mercer chose to build with reinforced concrete for several reasons. Both a subscriber and contributor to the magazine, Cement Age, he had presumably been reading about this material and was attracted by its fire-resistant qualities. He was interested in having a fireproof building to house his collections.

Yet he was also attracted by the plasticity of concrete, which his long experience with the plastic qualities of clay helped him appreciate. It was his firm belief that concrete could be molded into any shape and that it would stand forever. It was also particularly well-suited for the application of ceramic tile.

Under Mercer's constant direction, from eight to ten laborers mixed and poured the concrete for Fonthill. They were paid the prevailing wage of $1.75 per ten-hour day. The only other workers involved in the construction proper were Jacob Frank, an employee of the Moravian Pottery and Tile Works, who set the ceiling tiles, and a foreman. Afterward, however, Mercer used other skilled workers for finishing work: a carpenter worked on the doors, wooden windows, paneling and built-in furniture; a mason set the tiles in floors and walls; and a painter put in the window glass.

All of the concrete used to build Fonthill was mixed by hand, and was moved either in iron wheelbarrows or in boxes fitted with handles and carried by two men. As the house took shape, a horse named "Lucy" was trained to pull a rope attached to a pulley that lifted the concrete to the upper levels.

Fonthill actually began as a 1742 stone farmhouse, which was on the property when Mercer purchased it. It

43

became the kitchen and the dividing space between the main house and the servants' quarters. Mercer raised the roof to gain a full third floor, modified its interior to suit his design, then completely encased the old farmhouse in concrete.

This kind of "recycling" was typical of Mercer. He used salvaged materials throughout Fonthill. Old doors, for example, were used for interior paneling. Lumber for the concrete forms came from old buildings and an old bridge, while iron reinforcing pipes were bought at local junkyards. And used hardware was recycled wherever possible. Fonthill's outer walls rest on concrete footings five feet deep, and are three feet thick at the foundation. They taper up to a thickness of approximately 18" at the top and contain a 12" air space. This air space, which serves both as insulation and as a conduit for pipes and wires, was created by shaping the walls around forms that were later collapsed and removed.

The interior partitions of the house were cast five inches thick. In order to achieve an "aged" look, old boards with cracks and holes were purposely used in the forms to give the surface of the concrete a random, uneven texture.

Concrete columns supporting the roof slopes and upper-story partitions rise from the cellar to the housetop. There is no symmetrical arrangement to these columns, and one column, Mercer noted, "was cut off during construction in the yellow room to make way for a bed."

The forms for these columns were made of boards placed vertically and held together in circles with rope and wire, or in squares with battens. Each column was reinforced with three vertical ¾" hollow iron pipes, plus wire circles that were twisted by hand and dropped down the forms about two feet apart as the concrete was poured. The tiled capitals and bases of the columns were set after construction.

Beams for the house were cast in normal formwork, and reinforced with six solid iron rods. Galvanized rectangular-mesh farm fencing was laid over all reinforcing steel. To achieve a molded shape in some beams, long ropes of clay were tamped into the lower corners of the beam form.

PLVS VLTRA

1. View of Fonthill
2. Gallery
3. Detail of New World tiles on the Library fireplace

45

1. Dormer Room Bath
2. Bedroom
3. Window detail in Columbus Room
4. Morning Room Fireplace

Photographs ©1998 Alan Karchmer

The Columbus Room ceiling depicts the exploration and discovery of the New World

1. Fonthill's unusual roofline
2. The Saloon
3. Sunlight washes across tiles on the Russian Stove
4. Mercer's pottery collection in the study
5. Stairs to the Columbus Room

Photographs ©1998 Alan Karchmer

1. Pickwick Fireplace in the West Room
2. Dormer Room Bath
3. Yellow Room Stairs
4. Detail of frame of mirror of dresser (note exposed light bulb)

A curved wire was then used to cut a trough in the clay, into which the wet concrete settled and set into a rounded bead.

Mercer devised an ingenious method for constructing his vaulted ceilings and installing the decorative ceiling tiles. Instead of the complicated carpentry it would have taken to create curved forms, he erected wooden platforms across the top of a room between the columns. On top of these platforms, piles of dirt were shaped to correspond to the curves of the ceiling he wanted. Once these dirt mounds were properly molded, they were covered with a final layer of sand.

The decorative tiles were then positioned and pressed face down into the sand, with about a quarter of an inch left projecting out. Wire mesh and pipe reinforcing was laid over the tiles, and the entire mass was then covered with concrete, which formed the floor of the room immediately above as well. After the concrete had hardened, Mercer wrote, "when we pulled out the platforms props, the platforms collapsed and tons of earth and sand fell, exposing the tiles, after which the loose sand was washed off with a hose and when dry, (the concrete was) brushed and shellaced between the tiles."

This unique method of using earth mounds to form his ceilings saved Mercer a great deal of time and expense. If the same had been decorated in the usual manner – that is, setting the tiles onto the surface of already hardened concrete vaults – each ceiling would have taken about two weeks to complete. With Mercer's method, however, a ceiling, with all its intricate design, could be created in just a few days.

Although Mercer constructed Fonthill to look like a medieval castle, he also wanted it to have all the modern conveniences available in 1910. These included plenty of indoor plumbing, a complicated central heating system, and electric lights.

Mercer carefully planned the plumbing at Fonthill, and created a unique system to get enough water pressure for all the bathrooms and lavatories he wanted.

From a pumphouse under the West Spring Terrace, a gas-powered pump (later converted to electricity)

Fireplace in the Smoking Room

transferred water from an artesian well to the top of the tower via a series of pipes. There, the water was stored in large cisterns.

These cisterns were built of concrete. To make them as water-tight as possible, alum was added to the concrete before the cisterns were cast, and a "water-proof" cement was used to coat the tanks.

From the cisterns, water was then piped down to the bathrooms and sinks of the house. The force of gravity from the top of the tower to the lower portions of the house increased water pressure to these facilities.

To heat Fonthill, Mercer resorted to several different methods, which he developed from research conducted before construction began.

First, he built fireplaces into almost every room, except the West Room, Map Room, and Dormer Room. Some fireplaces have large valves next to them, which was one way Mercer devised to improve the flow of hot air through the room. Cool air coming through open windows in the basement would be heated by duct work. When the valve was opened, this heated air would rise behind the fireplace and displace the heat from the flames, forcing warm air out into the room more effectively.

Three coal furnaces in the basement provided a second method of heating Fonthill. These furnaces, replaced by oil furnaces in 1937, produced "direct" and "indirect" steam heat. In the direct system, water was heated in boilers for the steam radiators throughout the house. The indirect system involved the vents that open in the walls of some of the rooms. Air was heated over a system of radiators and coils in the basement, and this hot air traveled up through piping and duct work to exit out all the wall vents.

Russian stoves were also used as a source of heat in the Saloon and the Breakfast Room. Mercer, who said he got the idea from Russian immigrants, covered these wood stoves with his own tiles. When a fire was built in the stove, the tiles became very hot and radiated heat out into the room.

Soon after the basic construction was complete, Fonthill glowed with electric light. The original wiring and more than half the lights were installed in 1910. More lights were added along with a new generator in 1921, but there were never any outlets or fixtures. Fonthill's bell-call system was installed in 1910 by the same electrician who did the wiring for the lights; he also put in the house phones in 1921.

Today, Fonthill has new wiring with a higher capacity and modern insulation. Except for this, however, it is completely authentic in style and appearance to the original. The paired, braided lampcords with brass sockets and naked carbon filament bulbs look exactly as they did when the initial wiring was installed by Mercer's electrician.

The Dormer Room, with decorative tiles in ceiling arches

5

A Home for Treasures

The Columbus Room

A Home for Treasures

Although how Henry Mercer designed and built his dream home is fascinating in itself, the real fascination of Fonthill lies in the decorative tilework that embellishes every room.

The ceramic tiles that adorn Fonthill are a blend of tiles designed and created by Mercer himself, and tiles he collected from other countries. Many of the tiles installed as the house was constructed were produced at Mercer's first Moravian Pottery and Tile Works in Doylestown.

By far the most dramatic tilework in Fonthill is found on the intricate and extremely elaborate ceilings of the Columbus Room and the Bow Room.

In the Columbus Room, the entire ceiling is covered with richly colored tiles depicting scenes of the discovery of the New World. There are seven large panels in all, each made up of smaller triangles illustrating everything from maps by Leonardo da Vinci to scenes of Columbus leaving Spain and arriving in the West Indies. There are even references to Cortez, Ponce de Leon, Pizarro in Peru, and Indian cannibals. Most of these scenes were adapted from 16th century woodcuts.

Mercer also paid tribute to Columbus on the floor of this room. These words, from a poem about Columbus by Joachim Miller, appear in tile letters around the floor's perimeter:

"Brave Adm'r'l, speak but one good word;
What shall we do when hope is gone?
The words leapt like a leaping sword:
Sail on! Sail on! Sail on! and on!"

There is so much to see on the Columbus ceiling that the eye hardly knows where to begin. Even Mercer himself admitted that he may have overdone it a little in this room. Yet that did not keep him from continuing the New World theme in the adjoining Bow Room, where the entire ceiling is a huge illustration in tile of a map of ancient Mexico City.

Throughout Fonthill, Mercer used tile to add personal touches of philosophy and humor to his home. On fireplaces and stair risers he placed mottos and phrases that often had double meanings.

In the Library, for example, the fireplace bears the phrase, "Plus Ultra", meaning "More Beyond", and the stairs to the Saloon read "per Varios Casus" (translated: "Through many changes of fortune") – the motto from the Mercer family coat of arms. While in the Morning Room, the fireplace bears the words "Ardet Fortuna", meaning "Fortune Ablaze." Similar Latin phrases appear throughout the house, including this message on the Terrace Room skylight: "Post Nubila Phoebus," or "Beyond the clouds, the sun."

Mercer also placed messages in English. Upstairs, in the Yellow Room, the stairs to the bathroom say "Best for the West." This has a double meaning, for the room not only looks best in the western light of late afternoon, but those particular stairs are also the best way to get to the west side of the house. Mercer used a play on words in the Dormer Room bathroom, as well: around the walls is an Irish greeting – "The Top of the Morning." Yet the Dormer Bath also happens to be directly over the Morning Room, making it "The Top of the Morning Room."

Mercer even immortalized his dog, Rollo, a big Chesapeake Bay retriever. While the stairs leading up from the Columbus Room were being cast, Rollo apparently ran up the wet cement. Instead of smoothing out the paw prints, Mercer let the cement harden with Rollo's signature intact, and added tile letters which announce forever that these are "Rollo's Stairs."

For inspiration for his tile designs, Mercer turned to many sources. Quite early in his tile making, Mercer took designs from the Pennsylvania German stoveplates he collected. These stoveplates bore pictorial scenes – mostly Biblical in nature, and often illustrating moral lessons. Mercer pressed clay onto the raised metal designs of the stoveplates, then made plaster molds which were used to shape the tiles. Many of the tile pictures in the Saloon, particularly on the ceiling beams and Russian stove, were taken from the stoveplates.

Another major design source for Mercer's Fonthill tiles were woodcuts, engravings and etchings, especially those which illustrated a book he owned: A Narrative and Critical History of America. Many of the New World scenes in the Columbus and Bow Rooms were adapted from these illustrations.

Mercer also used prints and other artwork as sources for tile designs, and occasionally translated images from fabrics. The pattern above the Morning Room fireplace is taken from a 16th century Italian tapestry. The "brocade" tiles on the Russian stove in the Breakfast Room were derived from a Persian pattern book in a museum in England. Mercer also reproduced parts of a Spanish chest, a carved wooden box, and a brass Persian tray in tile.

Mercer collected designs from other tiles, as well, especially from the medieval period. Some of the ceiling mosaics in the Study seem to be enlargements of similar relief tiles made at Toledo, Spain, in the 16th or 17th century. The floor of the Map Room is composed of reproductions of medieval tiles. And the tiles in the Yellow Room depicting a castle and an eagle were taken from two tiles excavated at the Church of Santa Maria, Seville, Spain.

Many of Mercer's tile designs, however, cannot be traced to a particular source. And even if they could, his own imagination and artistic ability left them with a quality all their own. Mercer's Indian mosaics and the tiles depicting everyday activities are entirely unique, while some Mercer tiles resemble Wedgwood pottery – unglazed blue and white raised designs.

In addition to his own tiles, Mercer installed many different examples of foreign tiles at Fonthill. Since Fonthill was also to be a museum, he wanted to present an illustrated history of tile-making throughout the world.

Mercer officially began this collection of tiles in 1914, and most were purchased through correspondence. He would obtain the names of Presbyterian missionaries around the world and send each a form letter, asking if the country they were in had a history of tile-making. He also wrote to military officers and YMCA workers in various countries.

Rollo's Stairs in the Columbus Room

Through these contacts, he acquired the tiles and tools which are displayed on the Chinese Roof Tile Balcony, as well as others.

Mercer also purchased tiles from dealers in New York City and elsewhere. The Dutch and Persian tiles were obtained in this manner, and the Spanish tiles were purchased from a dealer in Gibraltar.

The origins of Mercer's foreign tiles span the globe, including Mexican, European, Asian and Middle Eastern examples dating from the 13th to the 19th century. Most of the foreign tiles at Fonthill have numbers on them, which were added by Mercer himself – he kept a catalog of his collection.

From the first, Fonthill served as a kind of an advertisement for Mercer tiles, since Mercer installed most of the different kinds of tiles he produced. The "story" tiles (such as the tale of Bluebeard in the Yellow Room and the tiles illustrating the Pickwick Papers) were very popular in their own time for use around fireplaces. Mercer even designed a series of golfing tiles when he was commissioned by a country club, and he installed examples of these in one of Fonthill's bathrooms.

In fact, the whole time Henry Mercer resided at Fonthill he was adding tiles – both of his own making and those he collected. He set the tiles on the walls, the ceilings, the fireplaces, and anywhere else he could find space. The Gallery offers an example of Mercer's later tilework. He was in the process of completing it when he died and only two of the four seasons of the year are represented. Whether he might have done more if space and time had permitted remains an unsolved puzzle.

In addition to his tiles, Mercer also used his vast collection of prints to decorate his home. Nearly 1,000 framed prints hang from the walls of Fonthill, and albums or "folios" stacked in rooms throughout the house contain more than 6,000 additional unframed pictures.

The majority of these prints represent the works of great artists, and were published in England between 1750 and 1850. The rest are from Italy, Germany, France and America.

Tiles, artifacts and prints from Italy, Germany,

Altogether, Mercer's collection of prints spans a period from the early 16th century to the early 20th century.

France and America adorn the Saloon

Photograph Courtesy Barry Halkin

6

A Treasure
for All to Share

Photograph © Edward Eckstein

Fonthill

70

A Treasure
for All to Share

Henry Mercer lived at Fonthill from May of 1912 until his death in 1930. During that time, he entertained many distinguished visitors at his home, opening the doors of Fonthill to such notable figures as John Phillip Sousa, Marcel Duchamps, Victor Herbert and Henry Ford.

While some of Mercer's famous visitors stayed at Fonthill itself, Henry Ford did not. As the story goes, Ford wanted to establish his own museum in Michigan, and offered Mercer a million dollars for his collection of artifacts. Miffed that Ford had even suggested such an idea, Mercer allowed Ford to visit Fonthill, but made him stay at a local hotel.

Upon his death, Mercer's will left Fonthill to the public "...as a museum for the exhibition and study of decorative tiles, decorative art, of engravings and woodcuts, and of the technical and artistic processes of concrete house construction."

Mercer's will also granted life occupancy of Fonthill to Frank Swain (Manager of the Moravian Pottery and Tile Works) and his wife, Laura, who was Mercer's housekeeper. Laura Swain maintained and conducted private tours of Fonthill until just before her death in 1975, at which time the Bucks County Historical Society began operating Fonthill as a public museum.

Today Fonthill stands as a monument to its builder's artistic vision, his inventiveness, and his ability to go beyond conventional solutions. As such, it is more than just a house made of concrete. It is a highly personal blend of romanticism and ingenuity, an expression on the grandest scale of the individual tastes, beliefs, and intriguing visions of Henry Chapman Mercer.

Henry Mercer's Construction Notebook for Fonthill

Henry Mercer's creativity and genius are reflected everywhere at Fonthill. No architectural concept was too broad for him to consider; no construction detail was too small for his attention. Both the small and broad strokes of the artist in concrete are abundantly evident in the composition-size notebook that he used during the building of his new home.

Mercer's construction notebook is a fascinating source of information about what was built and what was not; which names were considered and which survived. From the height of the ceilings to the thickness of the walls, from the proportions of the tower roof to the tile decoration in the halls, the notebook reflects Mercer's unique and very personal approach to the construction.

The photographs that follow are of entire pages in Mercer's construction notebook, part of the collection of the Bucks County Historical Society.

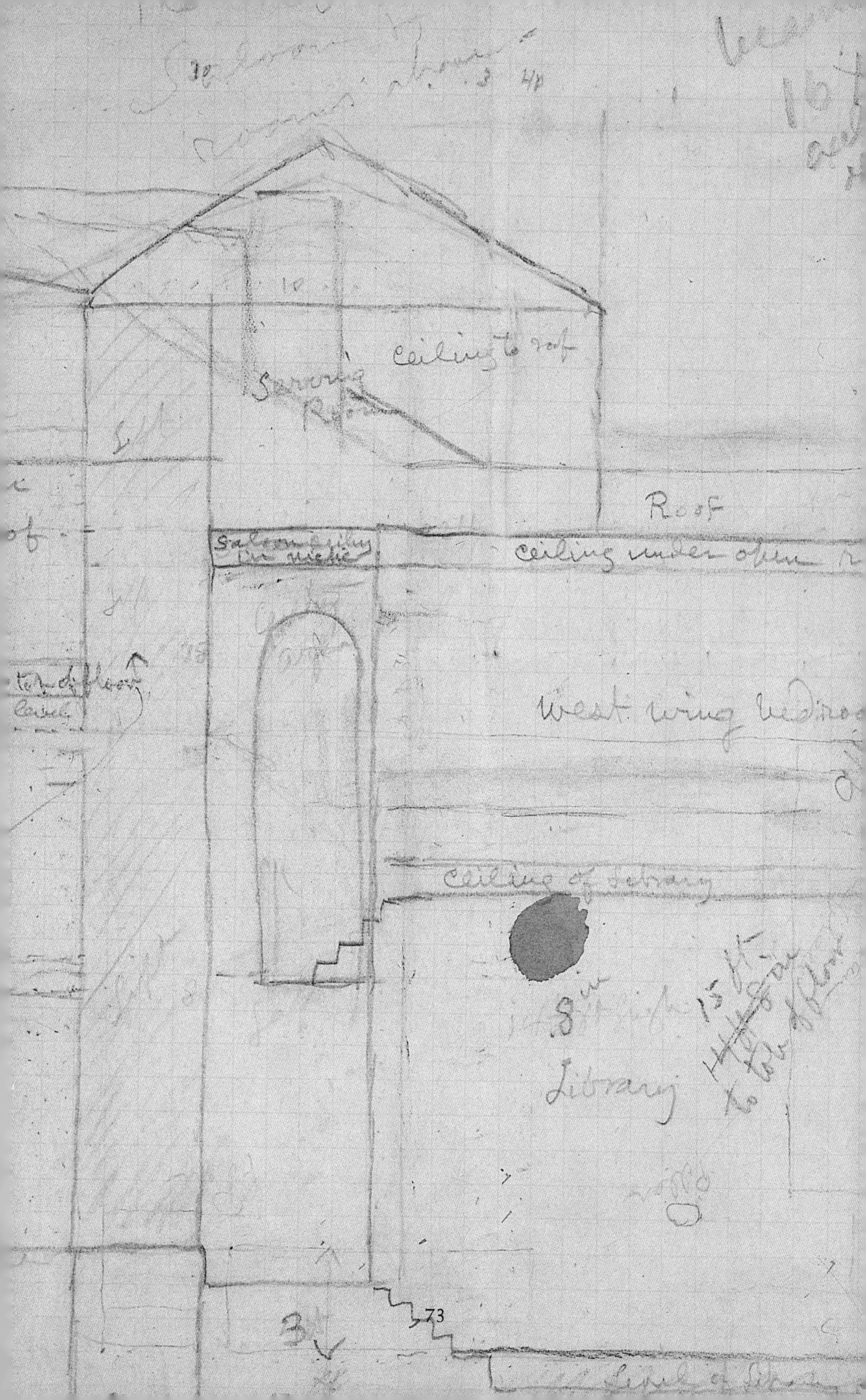

ceiling to roof

Serving
Room

Saloon gilly
in niche

Roof
ceiling under open r

West wing bedroo

ceiling of library

8 " high 15 ft

Library

73

3

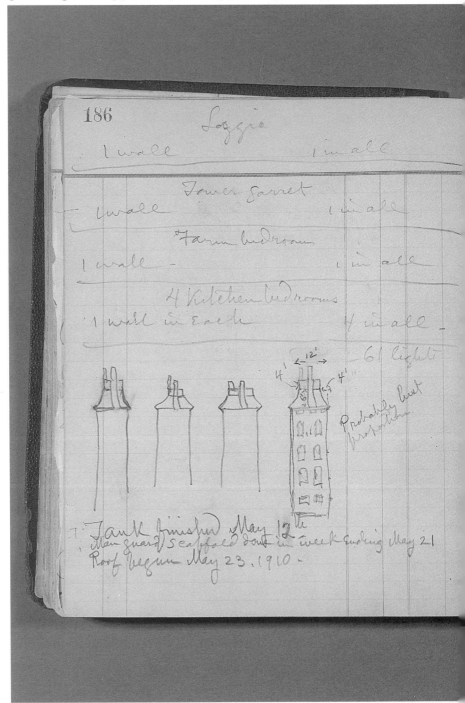

186

Loggia

1 wall   1 in all

Tower garret

1 wall   1 in all

Farm bedroom

1 wall -   1 in all

4 Kitchen bedrooms

1 wall in Each   4 in all -

                                          61 lights

Probably best
proportion

7. Tank finished May 12th
Man guard Scaffold down in week ending May 21
Roof begun May 23, 1910 -

Basic design variations for Fonthill's Tower (pencil and pen on paper, 7"x8½")

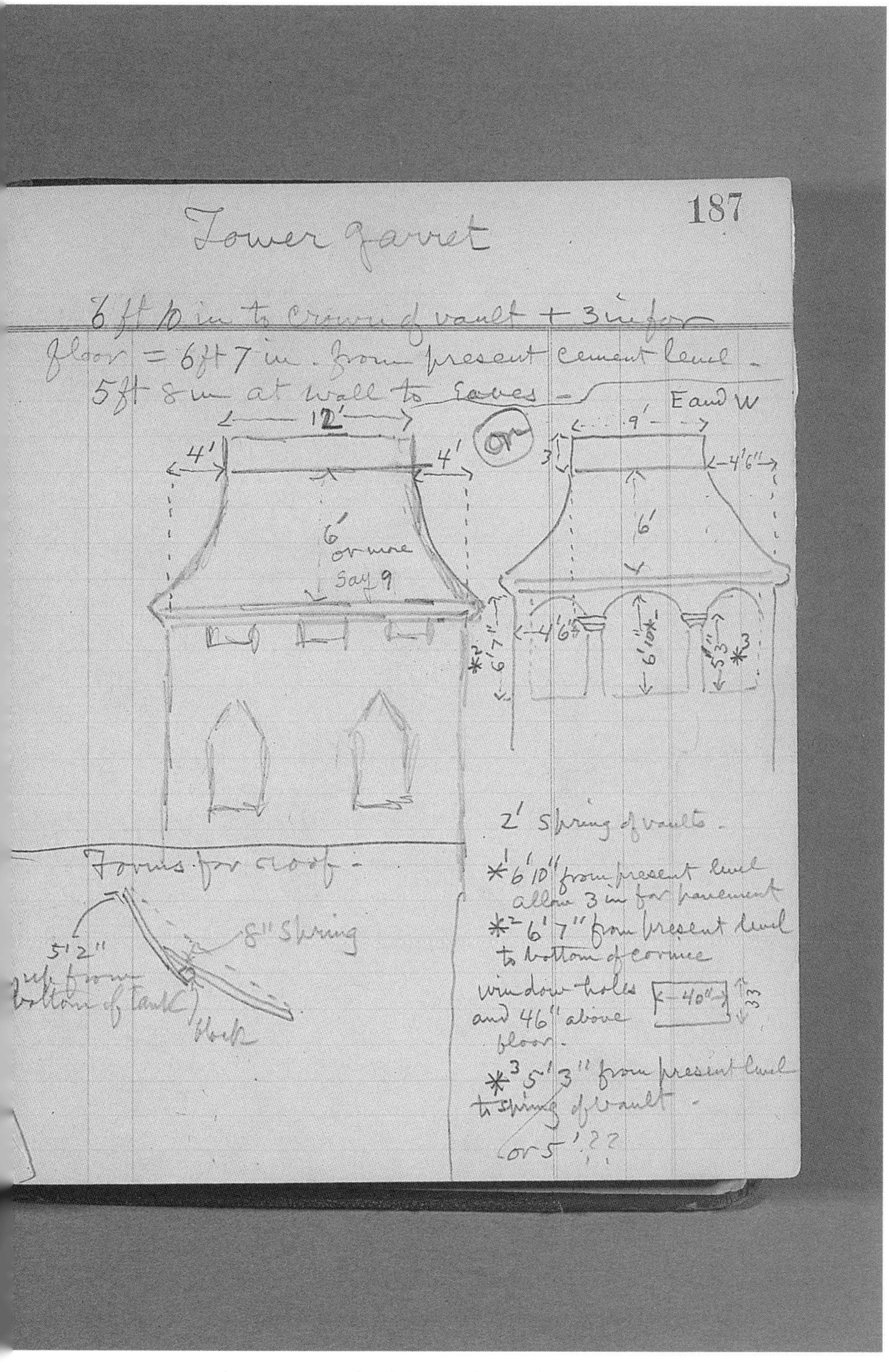

187

Tower garret

6 ft 10 in to crown of vault + 3 in for
floor = 6 ft 7 in. from present cement level –
5 ft 8 in at wall to eaves –

E and W

2' spring of vaults –

*¹ 6' 10" from present level
allow 3 in for pavement

*² 6' 7" from present level
to bottom of cornice

window holes
and 46" above
floor –

*³ 5' 3" from present level
to spring of vault –
or 5' ??

Forms for roof –

5' 2"
left from
bottom of tank

8" spring

brick

Details of design alternatives

75

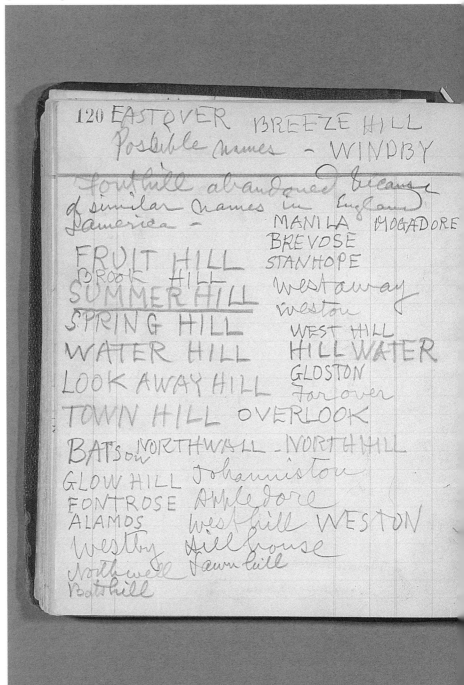

120 EASTOVER   BREEZE HILL
Possible names - WINDBY

Fonthill abandoned because
of similar names in England
& america -   MANILA MOGADORE
                BREVOSE
FRUIT HILL   STANHOPE
BROOK HILL
SUMMER HILL   westaway
SPRING HILL   weston
                WEST HILL
WATER HILL   HILL WATER
LOOK AWAY HILL   GLOSTON
                farover
TOWN HILL OVERLOOK
BATSon NORTHWALL - NORTH HILL
GLOW HILL Johanniston
FONTROSE Appledore
ALAMOS   westhill WESTON
westby   Hillhouse
Northwell Fawnhill
Bathill

Mercer considered many names before finally selecting "Fonthill" despite initially rejecting it

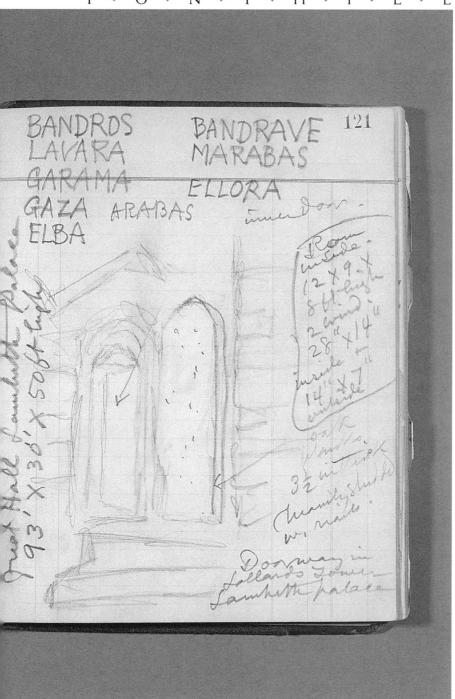

BANDROS   BANDRAVE   121
LAVARA   MARABAS
GARAMA   ELLORA
GAZA   ARABAS
ELBA

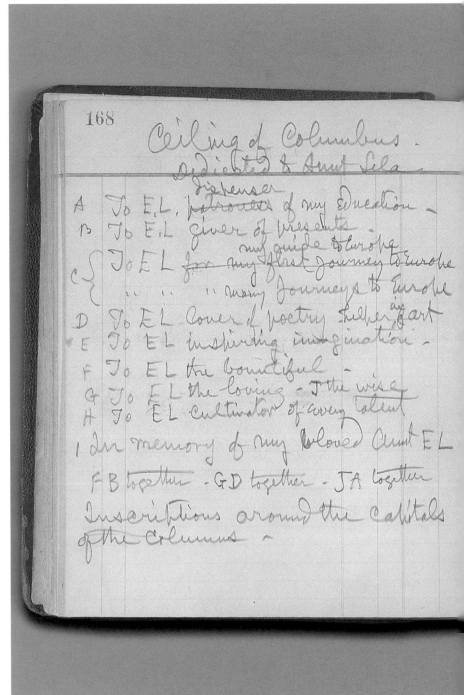

Mercer dedicated the Columbus Room to his Aunt Lela

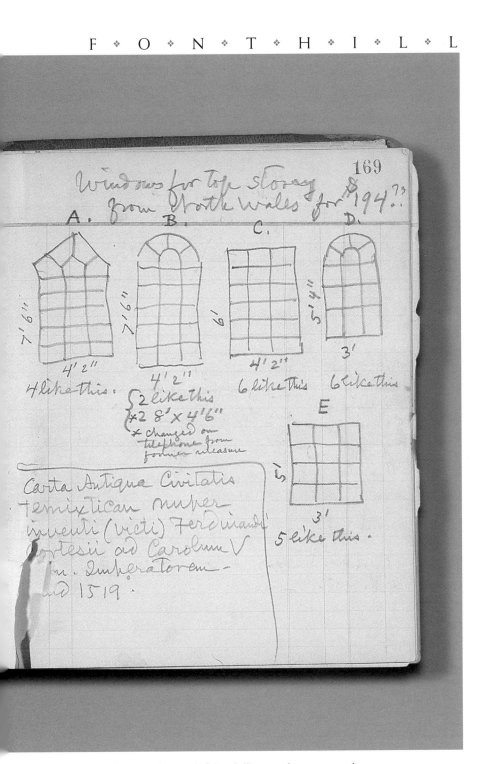

Specifications for some of Fonthill's more than 200 windows

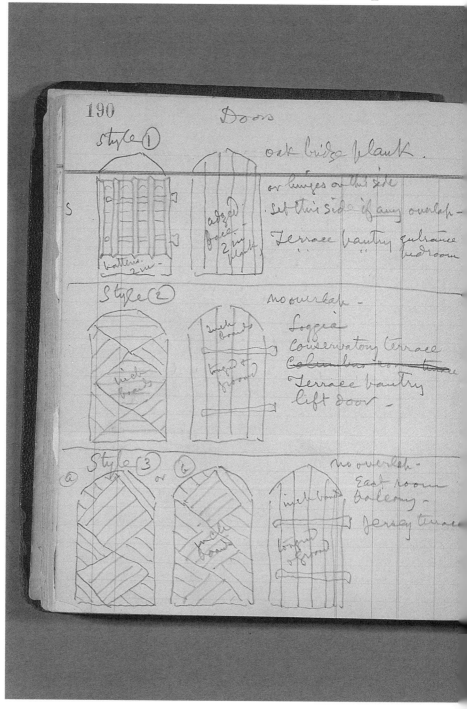

Some of the many door styles that were custom-built for Mercer's home

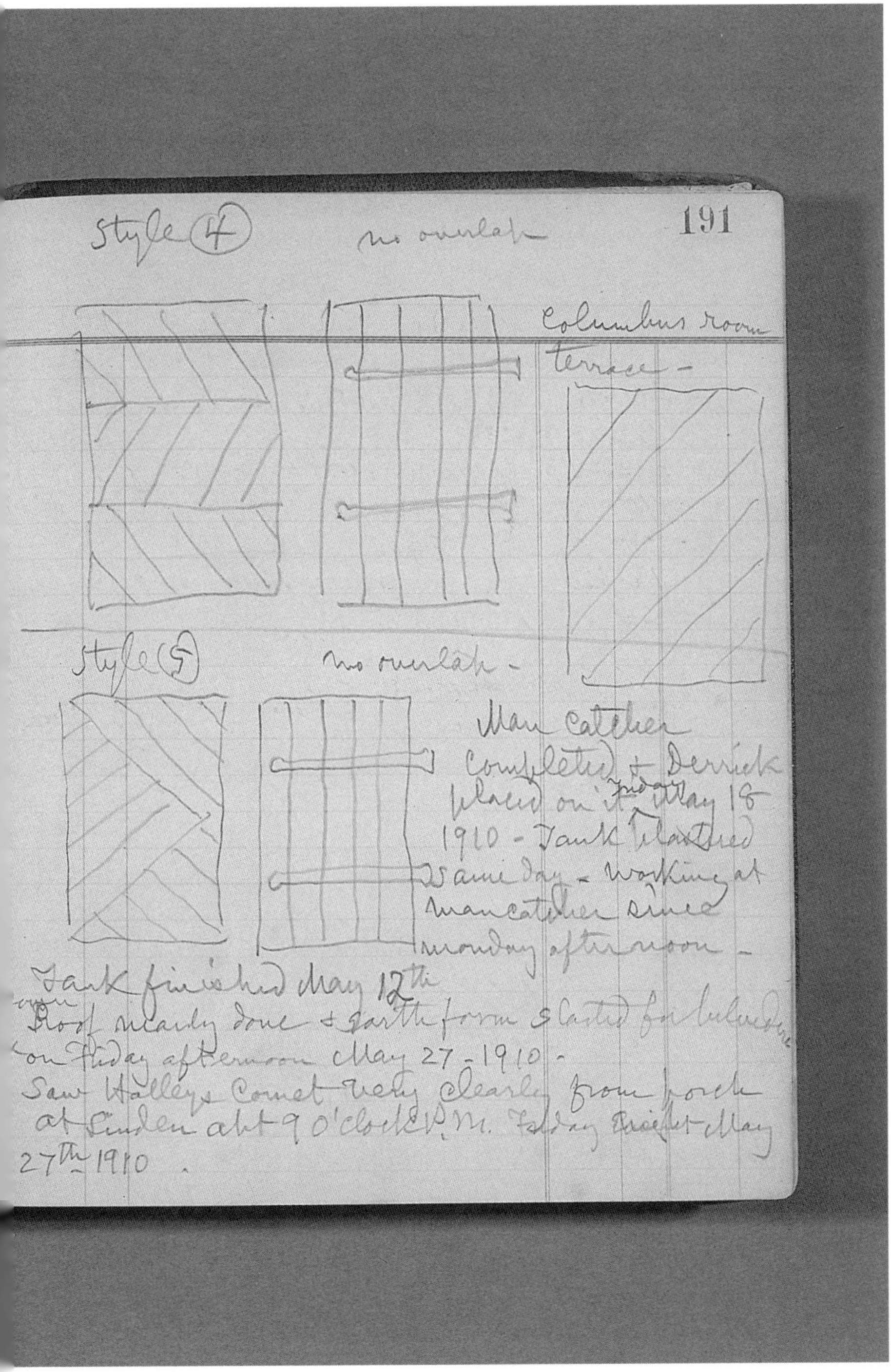

Style ④   no overlap   **191**

Columbus room

terrace —

Style ⑤   no overlap —

Man catcher
Completed + Derrick
placed on it 2nd May 18
1910 — Tank Plastered
Same day — working at
man catcher since
monday afternoon —

Tank finished May 12th

Roof nearly done + earth form started for bulwark[?]
on Friday afternoon May 27 - 1910 —
Saw Halley's Comet very clearly from porch
at Linden abt 9 O'clock P.M. Friday Night May
27th 1910 .

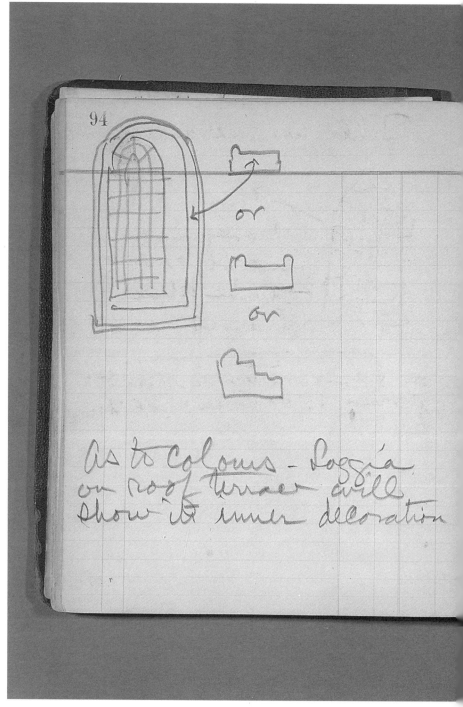

As to Colours - Loggia on roof terrace will show its inner decoration

Detail of window construction

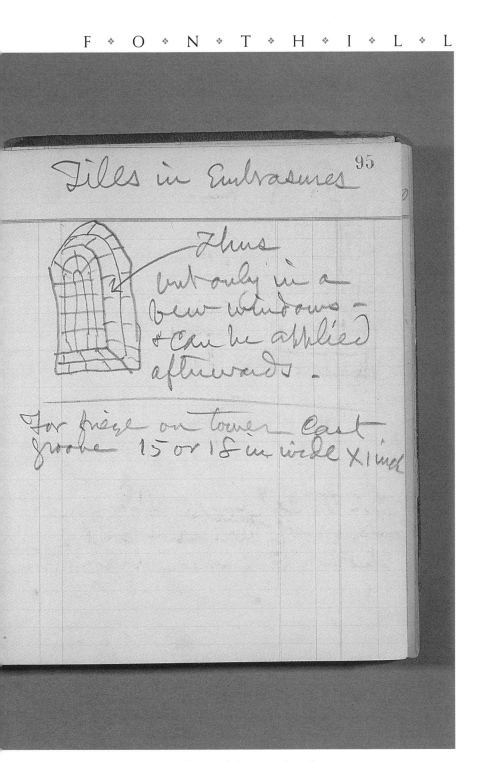

Plans for installation of tiles around windows

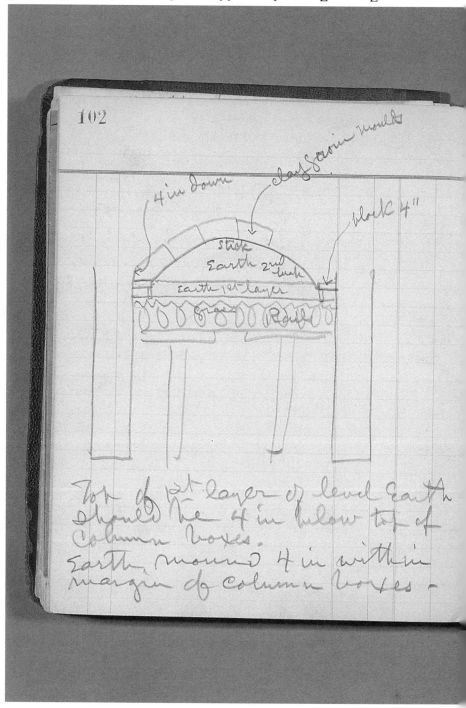

Construction detail for creating vaulted ceiling

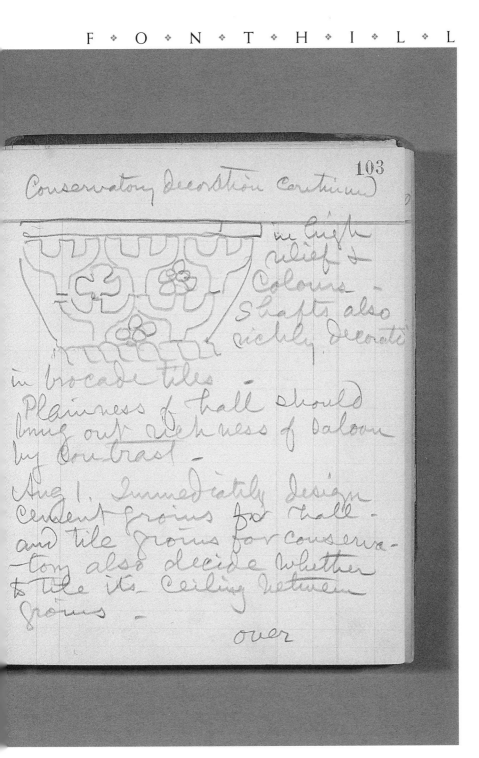

Conservatory decoration continued

in high relief & Colours –

Shafts also richly decorate

in brocade tiles

Plainness of hall should bring out richness of Saloon by Contrast –

Aug 1, Immediately design Cement groins for hall – and tile groins for conservatory also decide whether to tile its Ceiling between groins –

over

Highlights of design decisions and decorating alternatives

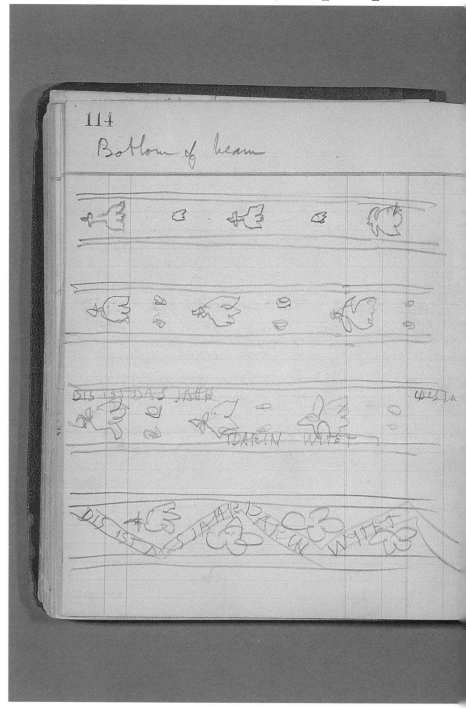

Designs for beam decoration

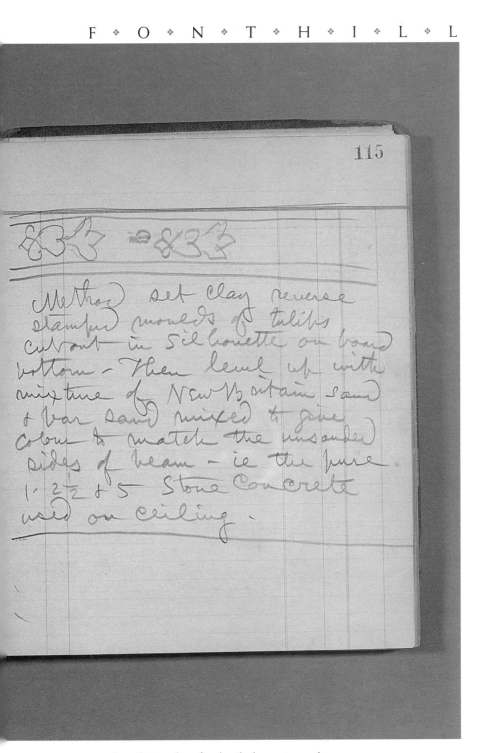

Installation plans for the tile decoration on beams

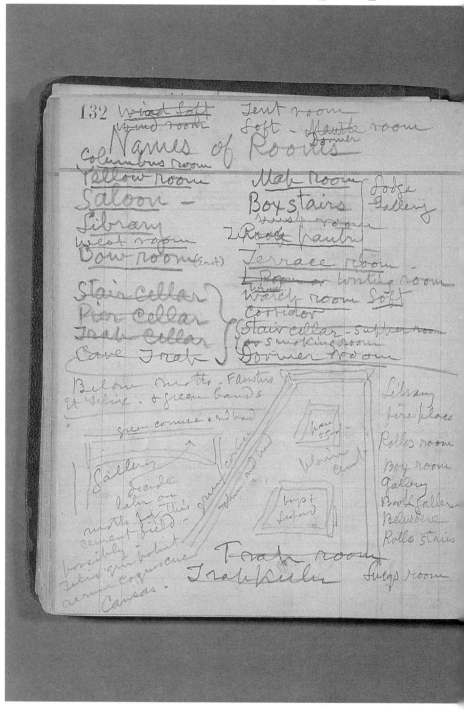

Potential names for rooms

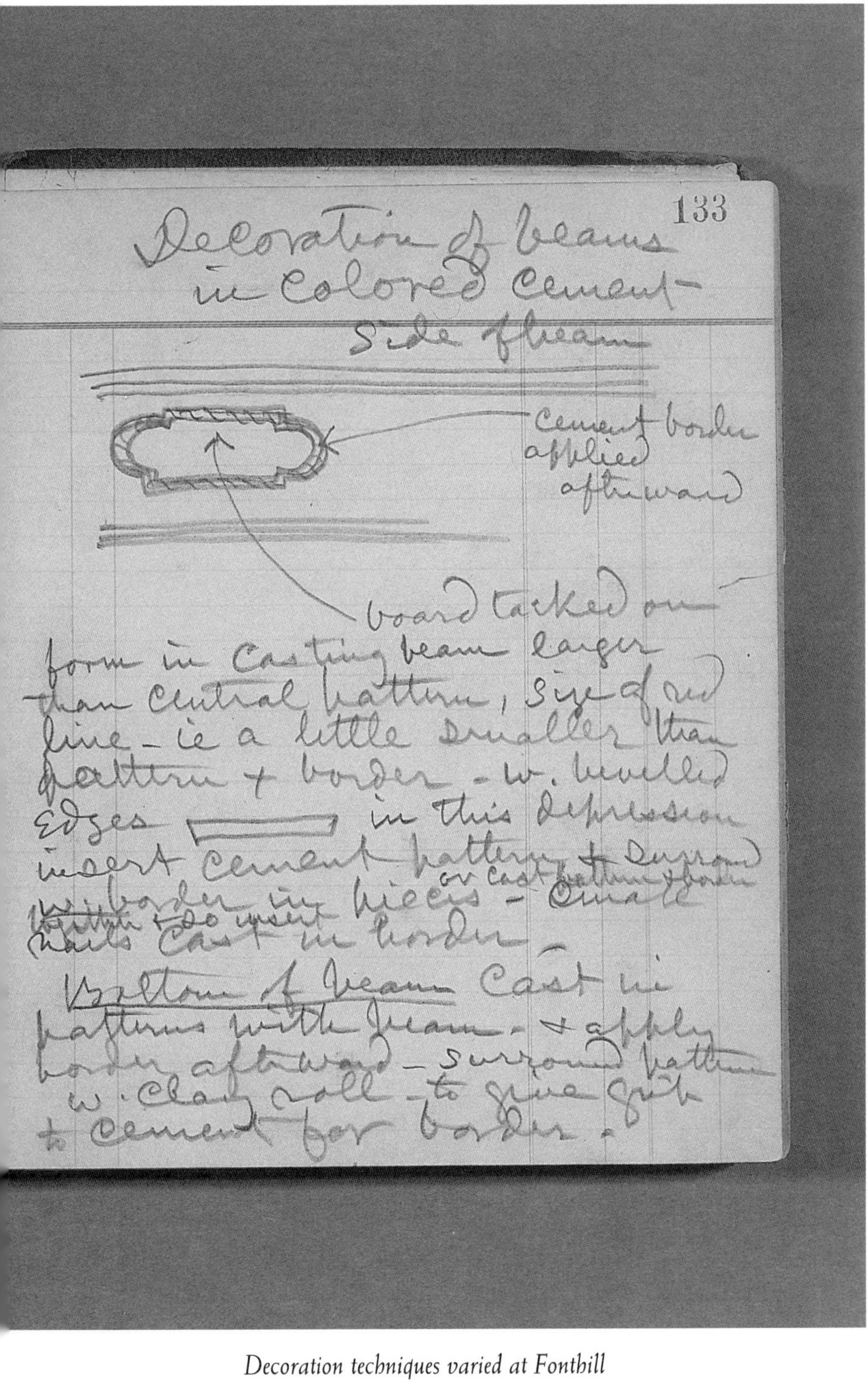

133

Decoration of beams
in colored cement –
Side of beam

cement border
applied
afterward

board tacked on

form in casting beam larger
than central pattern, size of red
line – ie a little smaller than
pattern + border – w. bevelled
edges in this depression
insert cement pattern + surround
w. border in pieces – small
(or cast pattern + border)
nails cast in border –

Bottom of beam cast in
patterns with beam – + apply
border afterward – surround pattern
w. clay roll – to give grip
to cement for border.

Decoration techniques varied at Fonthill

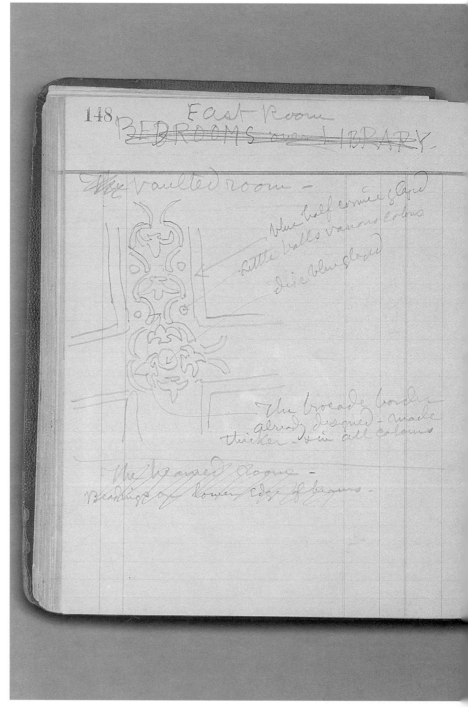

Tile design for the East Room ceiling

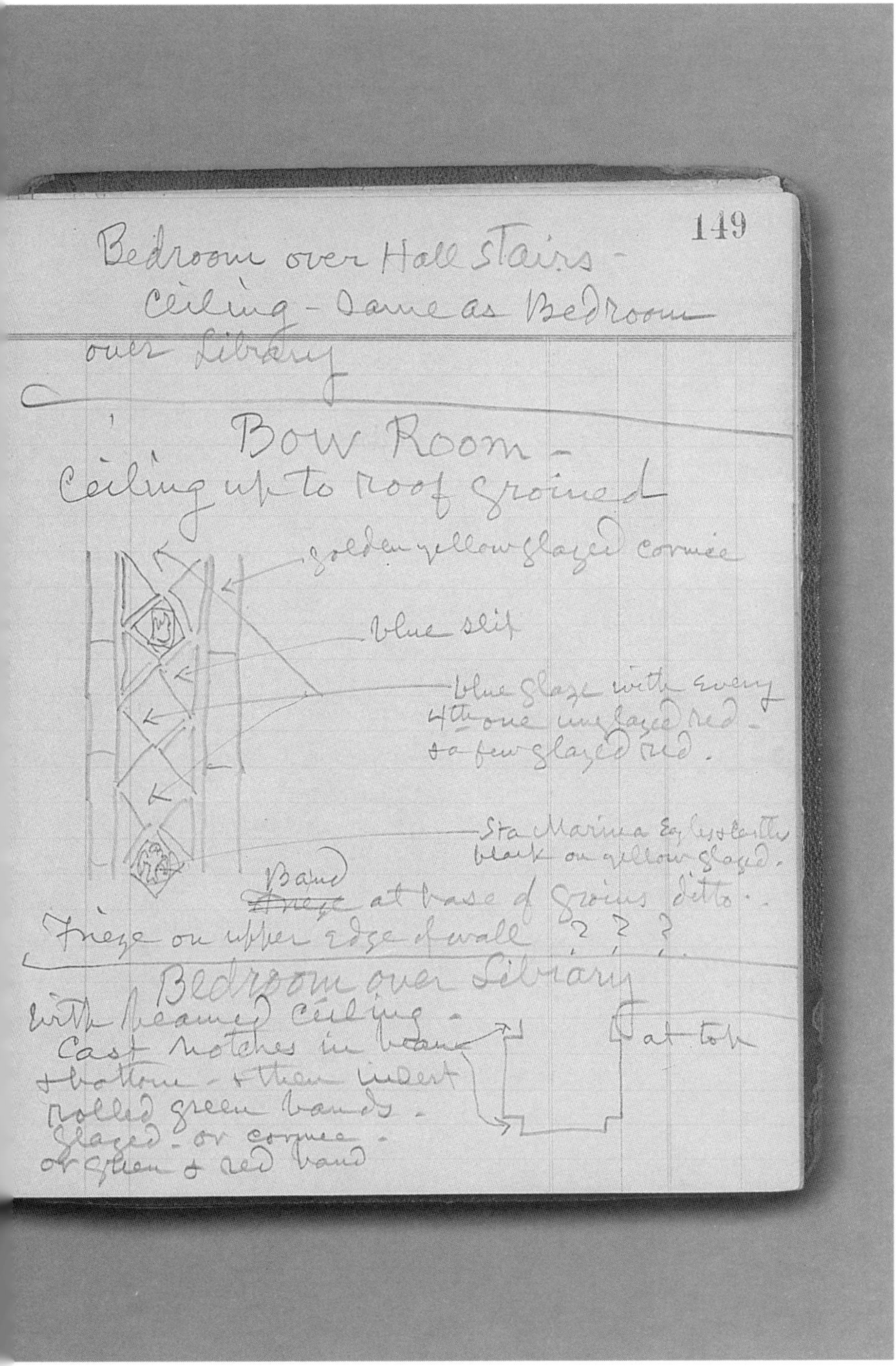

149

Bedroom over Hall Stairs –
Ceiling – Same as Bedroom
over Library

Bow Room –
Ceiling up to roof groined

golden yellow glazed cornice

blue slip

blue glaze with every
4th one unglazed red –
& a few glazed red.

Sta Marina Eagles & teeth
black on yellow glazed.

~~Frieze~~ Band at base of groins ditto.
Frieze on upper edge of wall ? ? ?

Bedroom over Library
with beamed ceiling –
Cast notches in beams
& bottom – & then insert
rolled green bands –
Glazed – or cornice –
or green & red band

Tile type and color choices were important

Design concepts for the capitals of the columns at Fonthill

Credits for Photography and Illustrations

The following professionals and organizations have generously given their permission to use their work in this book.

Color Photography

Alan Karchmer - Front cover; all photographs pp. 46 - 51; large photo p. 52, small photo p. 97

Scott Dorrance - Photographs #2, 3, 4 p. 52

Black and White Photography

Barry Halkin - Photograph pp. 66 - 67

Ed Eckstein - Photograph p. 70

Note 1 - All other photographs of Fonthill and Henry Mercer are courtesy of Fonthill Museum.

Note 2 - All photographs of Henry Mercer's hand-drawn floor plans, cross sections and pages excerpted from Mercer's Construction Notebook were taken by Rick Urbanowski. They are all provided courtesy of Manor House Publishing Co., Inc.

Illustrations

Kurt Eichenburger - Cross section of Fonthill p. 33; floor plans pp. 34, 35, 37, 39

Note - All other cross sections, floor plans and illustrations are the work of Henry Mercer. They are used courtesy of Fonthill Museum, Spruance Library and The Bucks County Historical Society.

Acknowledgements

The publisher gratefully acknowledges the support, assistance and contributions of the following individuals and organizations in the preparation of this new and substantially expanded edition of *Fonthill—The Home of Henry Chapman Mercer:* David April, site administrator at Fonthill Museum; photographers Alan Karchmer, Scott Dorrance, Ed Eckstein, Barry Halkin and Rick Urbanowski; architect Kurt Eichenburger; the staff of the Spruance Library, The Mercer Museum and Fonthill Museum of The Bucks County Historical Society.

In the first edition, author Thomas G. Poos noted that the following writings were a rich resource for information embodied in his text:

Personal Architecture: The Evolution Of An Idea In The House of H.C. Mercer, Esq., Doylestown, PA, by W. T. Taylor, The Architectural Record, March, 1913.

Dr. Mercer's Concrete Extravaganza, by Ilse Meissner Reese, Progressive Architecture, October, 1960.

Poured Concrete Eclecticism, by William Kleinsasser, Connection, Fall, 1967.

Fonthill: Romanticism and ingenuity cast in reinforced concrete, by Roger Barnes, Fine Homebuilding, December, 1981/January, 1982.

Fonthill Reference Manual, by the Bucks County Historical Society, August 1984

The publisher is also pleased to acknowledge the lasting contribution of author Thomas G. Poos, whose text has formed a fine foundation for this revised and expanded work.

Destination Doylestown
Three Mercer Museums and a Library

Although Henry Chapman Mercer's eclectic interests obliged him to travel extensively throughout the world, he always returned to the place of his birth, Doylestown, Pennsylvania. Doylestown was the place where he felt most comfortable; he truly enjoyed living and working there.

Thus, when this historian, collector of art and artifacts and tile manufacturer, decided to construct his magnificent new home, Fonthill, he chose to build it on a property along East Court Street in Doylestown, in historic Bucks County.

Fonthill—the home of Henry Chapman Mercer

Mercer's castle in concrete stands today as he planned it, an architectural wonder and, "a museum of decorative tile and prints." Now administered by the Bucks County Historical Society, guided tours of Fonthill fascinate visitors of all ages and give insight into Mercer and his genius. Visitors see all of the wondrous features of Fonthill and its contents that are highlighted in this book—and more.

For tours and reservations call 215-348-9461 ext. 10; *www.fonthillmuseum.org.*

The Moravian Pottery & Tile Works

Located within several hundred yards of Fonthill is The Moravian Pottery and Tile Works, which Mercer completed in 1912. The Tile Works, which is also constructed of reinforced concrete, served as Mercer's production facility for the multitude of decorative tiles for which he became so famous.

The Moravian Pottery and Tile Works is a wonderful place to visit as it reveals the artistic and business side of Henry Mercer's many talents. Built in the style of a Spanish mission, this one-story fireproof structure appears well suited to its purpose.

Visitors to the Tile Works have little difficulty imagining the activities that took place there, as it is operated as a living history museum today. Reproductions of the renowned Mercer tiles that decorate the walls, floors, fireplaces and ceilings of Fonthill and buildings throughout the world are now hand crafted by modern day artisans, much as they were in the past under Mercer's personal guidance.

In addition to watching artisans make tiles, visitors can tour the Tile Works and examine and purchase tiles made from the actual molds used in Mercer's day. The diversity of tiles on display in the showroom makes it an excellent place to shop for decorative tiles with which to begin one's own collection

The Mercer Museum

As an archeologist, historian, and collector of antiquity, Henry Mercer became concerned that the tools, implements and commonplace artifacts of early America might not survive to be appreciated by future generations. So he decided to use his creativity and wealth to personally ensure that the past would be both preserved and displayed for all Americans.

The result of his vision and effort is The Mercer Museum and its outstanding collection of tools, implements and artifacts used in America prior to 1850. More than 60 trades are represented. Furniture, folk art and many other items of the period are also among the thousands on display.

Mercer's entire collection of fascinating Americana is housed in the seven-story museum he constructed primarily of concrete. The structure, a National Historic Landmark, is located at 84 South Pine Street in Doylestown. The museum is open to visitors almost every day of the year.

The Spruance Library

Visitors to Fonthill, The Moravian Pottery & Tile Works or The Mercer Museum are often inspired to learn more about Mercer's life, his works, his collections or the locale where his productivity flourished. Thankfully, The Spruance Library, which is located on the third level of The Mercer Museum, is available and well staffed to meet such needs.

Spruance Library contains more than 25,000 books, diaries, manuscripts, photographs and special collections devoted to: Henry Mercer—his life, buildings, works, art and tiles; the trades and tools of pre-industrial America; the history and families of Bucks County. Mercer tiles depicting key events in Bucks County history are also on display.

For Further Information
The Bucks County Historical Society

The Bucks County Historical Society administers Fonthill, The Mercer Museum and The Spruance Library. The Society also maintains a well-stocked bookstore and small gift shop adjoining The Mercer Museum.

The Bucks County Historical Society is located at 84 South Pine Street, Doylestown PA 18901. The telephone number is 215-345-0210. The Web site is *www.mercermuseum.org*. The map below should prove helpful to visitors for the above-listed destinations in Doylestown.

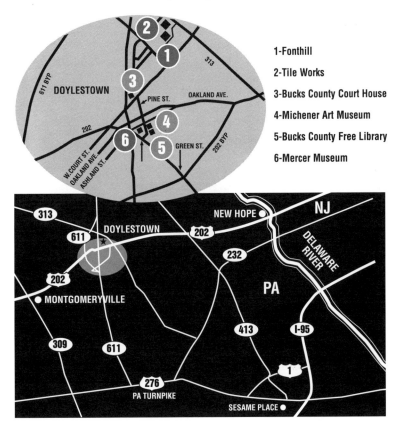

1-Fonthill

2-Tile Works

3-Bucks County Court House

4-Michener Art Museum

5-Bucks County Free Library

6-Mercer Museum

To order additional copies of

FONTHILL
The Home of Henry Chapman Mercer

from
Manor House Publishing Company
call
1-800-887-2011

between 9am and 5pm Eastern Time.
We accept Visa or Mastercard and we can usually ship
within 24 hours.

Fonthill Museum is a non-profit educational institution administered by the Bucks County Historical Society. A variety of programs are offered to the public, including regular guided tours and special programs for students. Fonthill is accredited by the American Association of Museums. For information: 215-348-9461.
For map, see page 99.

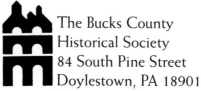 The Bucks County
Historical Society
84 South Pine Street
Doylestown, PA 18901

Fonthill Museum ❖ Spruance Library ❖ Mercer Museum

*"The construction was nowhere concealed.
From the first to the last, I tried to follow the precept...
decorate construction, but never
construct decoration."*

Henry Chapman Mercer